Frances Davies

Heart-Joys and Sorrows

Frances Davies

Heart-Joys and Sorrows

ISBN/EAN: 9783337777999

Printed in Europe, USA, Canada, Australia, Japan

Cover: Foto ©Thomas Meinert / pixelio.de

More available books at **www.hansebooks.com**

HEART-JOYS AND SORROWS.

BY
FRANCES DAVIES.

Manchester:
TUBBS & BROOK,
11, MARKET STREET.
MDCCCLXXIX.

PREFACE.

Go, wee pieces, into the world—
And if you've a mission there,
'Tis to speak of our Father, God,
And tell the worth of prayer.
But, if I have made a mistake,
And sent you abroad in vain;
My Father will over-rule it, I know,
And send you to me again.
And then I will ask Him to shew
The work He would have me to do;
But don't be afraid to come home,
There will be some work for you.

DEDICATION.

To the memory of my Mother,
I would dedicate this book :
Remembering all her gentle life,
And the loving pains she took
To point my heart and thoughts towards heaven :
And teaching me to see,
That I must give up my own self-will,
If I would be truly free.
That the riches she would have me seek,
Lay far away from here ;
The home I must fix my hopes upon,
Was in a different sphere.
Summer and winter will come and go,
 And have come many a time,
Since she left us, for her Father's home,
In that bright and happy clime.
She's passed away, from her earthly home,
But she speaketh, yet, to me :
And tells me to follow the footsteps
Of Him, whom I soon shall see.

CONTENTS.

	PAGE.
PREFACE	v.
DEDICATION	vii.
The Offering	1
The Invitation	3
Have you Answered the Door?	7
Will you come to the Master's Feast to-day?	10
The Promise	12
Will you be a Little Soldier? (Acrostic)	15
The Lord Bless Thee	17
The New Name	21
Fear not, I am with Thee	23
The New Year	25
Mamma, is this the way to Heaven?	26
The Angel and the Child	29
A Congratulation to Nellie	32
To the same, on her Marriage	34
The Neglected Message	36

CONTENTS.

	PAGE.
Passing Away	40
I will Trust in Thee	41
To Geraldine	43
To a Friend, on her Baptism	45
Times of Sorrow	49
To Nellie	51
Why art Thou cast down, my Soul?	55
Only a Baby, Nothing more	56
The Loss of the Princess Alice (In Memoriam)	58
In Memoriam	65
The Answered Letter	67
Hymn	69
God's Great Love to Man	72
Going Home	75
In Memoriam	76
In Memoriam	79
Good Night	81
Leave the Blinds a little while	84
Enter not into Temptation	87
The Journey of Life	90
In Memoriam	92
Farewell to England	94
Angel's Visit	96

CONTENTS.

	PAGE.
Jesus Wept	98
In Memoriam (Acrostic)	102
To Gracie	104
My Bible	106
Love Thy Neighbour as Thyself	108
Striving to do Thy will, Oh! God	110
In Memoriam	111
The Secret of the Lord	113
Work for the Women of England	114
The Blue Ribbon Army	117
Just Ten o'clock, on a Sabbath Eve	120
Who is to Blame?	122
The Hidden Path	125
Mamma, I saw you; Aunty, shall I see Jesus?	127
In Memoriam	130
Why did you give up your School?	132
Will you Write a Piece for my Album?	135
The Thorn in the Flesh	138
Conclusion	142

HEART-JOYS AND SORROWS.

THE OFFERING.

"And he looked up and saw the rich men casting their gifts into the Treasury."

I have so little I can bring,
A wilful, erring, foolish heart;
But as they each an offering place,
Oh! God, I want to do my part.

I have no wealth of any kind,
Of money, jewels, house, or land;
And thus I come before Thee, Lord,
With less than nothing in my hand.

For, looking back on years gone by,
They seem but wasted years to me;
And now I come with bitter cry,
And seek my all of help in Thee.

In love, take from my heart false shame,
And make me earnest in Thy work;
And every sin that hinders me,
That still within my soul would lurk.

Take Thou from me by any means,
Suffering, or shame, or sudden loss;
Till this I do, repeat Thy name,
And tell the story of the cross.

So make me useful in my day;
And if I cannot bring Thee gold,
Notice the offering, Lord, I pray,
As Thou did'st once to one of old.

And if a talent I have had,

And carelessly have kept it hid,

Forgiveness for the past, I crave,

And strength to do what Thou dost bid.

And now, my Father, I ask not

For wealth, or strength, or earthly fame;

I only ask for power, that I

May write and teach in Thy great name.

THE INVITATION.

"And they that were ready went in with Him, and the door was shut."

The Bridegroom has issued the invites,
    Said Edward, the brother, one day;
And the girls are anxiously waiting
    To hear what the mother will say.

The mother looked up from her reading,
    A bright smile illuming her face,
As she thought of her own loved daughters
    Receiving such wonderous grace.

For the bridegroom was rich and noble,
    A Prince, of King David's line ;
And the jewels he had to offer,
    For ever and ever would shine.

And the home in his Father's Kingdom
    Was glorious beyond compare ;
For sin with its blighting sorrow
    Was never allowed to come there.

So the maidens with eyes brightly gleaming,
    And hearts filled with tenderest love :
And lamps at the first surely burning,
    Set out for the kingdom above.

They thought all the way would be pleasant,
    That friends would encourage them on ;
That all would be kindness and honour,
    And envy and hatred be gone.

They knew not the master would tarry
    So long e'er he summoned them home :
Nor thought that the cross they must carry
    Before the bright crown could be worn.

So some of the maidens grew weary,
    And foolishly turned aside ;
Nor remembered the mighty honour
    In being the Saviour's bride.

But some of the maidens were faithful,
    And patiently waited their Lord ;
For to them the time passed more quickly,
    In carefully reading His word.

Oh ! there was dire confusion,
    In that dark deserted street,
And a sound of bitter wailing,
    As they came with trembling feet.

The Bridegroom come so suddenly,
    No warning given to them;
And scalding tears rain'd down their cheeks,
    For LOST the diadem

The bridegroom once has been on earth,
    Is coming once again;
An invite now he sends to thee,
    Oh ! hear it not in vain.

The trump will sound, the judge descend,
    To be your Master, or your friend;
The door is open wide to-night,
    May close before the morning light.

HAVE YOU ANSWERED THE DOOR?

"Behold, I stand at the door, and knock."

Have you answered the door?
Did you not hear a knock?
Or is your visitor poor,
One whom you fear not to mock?

If I were to tell you now,
He was a Prince in disguise,
How lowly would be your bow,—
What pride would flash in your eyes.

How soon the neighbours would see
Your doors thrown open wide;
And your highest pleasure would be
As He walked in by your side.

To honour your noble guest
With the best of all your food;
And beg Him to take some rest,
And study His every mood.

He came here without His gold:
He left His glory behind;
You see He had been told
He had priceless gems to find.

He had very much work to do,
And plenty of pain to bear;
And He only asks that you,
Do not add more to His care:

By your want of faith and love,
By your thoughtless, careless life;
By slighting the Holy Dove,
Who lived here amid such strife.

He came as a poor man here:
He brought not His wealth with Him;
He knew that sin's faithless fear
The brightest jewels would dim.

So up in the mansion's fair,
Placed there by His own dear hand,
Is the crown you will have to wear,
When you come to the better land.

He'll meet you quite at the door,
And take you up to the throne;
And then as you stand before,
The Father his child will own.

I told you He was a Prince:
He's more, He's King of glory;
You must believe on Him since
I have told you this true story.

Now you will open the door
And take Him into your heart,
And give Him of all your store,
The richest and sweetest part.

Never mind if He seems poor :
He's rich, the richest of Kings ;
You must taste, so bright and pure,
The joy such richness brings.

WILL YOU COME TO THE MASTER'S FEAST TO-DAY?

Will you come to the Master's feast to-day?
The tables are spread and the host will wait ;
But do not trifle the sunshine away,
Or perchance you will find yourselves too late.

There's a glad bright light and plenty to eat,
And every Christian will welcome you there ;
The Master Himself will give you a seat
And hand you the robe His children all wear.

It is spotless and white, and free from stain :
It should be, it's washed in the Saviour's blood :
And He'll make you pure and faultless again,
If you'll bathe yourselves in the tidal flood.

And angels are standing with beaming eyes,
To hear if you list to the Master's voice,
And follow His footsteps up to the skies,
The song in heaven would be Rejoice :—

Another has broken the bonds of sin,
Another accepted new life to-day ;
In the past, whatever your life has been,
In the future, you'll surely send a ray

Of Gospel light on some struggling soul,
And shew them what Jesus has done for you,—
How He healed the wounds and made you whole :
Oh ! speak for the Master you find so true.

THE PROMISE.

"I will never leave thee nor forsake thee."

They are precious words;
And in all their power
They came to me
In life's darkened hour.

For friends were but few,
And money all gone;
With nothing on earth
To lean upon.

As I sat and thought
What I should do next,
The angel came
And brought me the text.

And I knew at once
My Father above,
Had sent the message
In tenderest love.

So my heart grew light
With such holy joy,
That earth with its pain
Could never destroy.

I know I'm still poor,
As poor need be :
As far as the world
And worldings can see.

" I know thou art poor,"
God said in His word ;
" But my child thou art rich
In trusting thy Lord."

Then why need I fear
What losses may bring,
When my own Father
Is such a rich King.

And if He chooses
To give me my food
Each day as I need,
It still proves His love.

He knows the glitter
And tinsel of earth
Would draw my weak heart
From the heavenly birth.

He bids me be brave,
And faithfully stand,
Till He calls me home
To His own bright land.

And I mean to be,
If He gives me grace,
To do His dear will
E'er I see His face.

And when I go home
And bend near the throne,
I feel sure I shall know,
As now I am known.

WILL YOU BE A LITTLE SOLDIER?

(ACROSTIC.)

"Thou, therefore, endure hardness, as a good Soldier of Jesus Christ."

Will you be a little soldier,
In the army of our King?
Listening to His loving footsteps,
Leaving every sinful thing.

In the battle there'll be fighting,
And a very little boy
Must keep his weapons brightly shining,
Soon he'll find them full employ.

Nothing daunted, nothing fear,
As your Captain is quite near;
Pressing on you'll wear the prize,
Evermore beyond the skies.

Learn your work, now, little soldier,
You must go recruiting, too;
Now be thoughtful, patient, earnest,
Willing, lowly, work to do.

Often you will be in danger,
Often too by troubles pressed;
Don't despair you little stranger,
Learning here the King's behest.

Of giving all your heart and service,
Doing nothing but obey;
Going where the Bible bids you,
Ever wait the coming day.

All your work is now before you,
Going, coming, as you are told;
Every idol must be banished,
Dearer tho' it be than gold.

To your duty, little soldier,
Wait your great commander's smile:
Over you His angels watching,
Yearning o'er you here awhile.

Eager that your heart be given,
And at once in early youth;
Reaching forth your hand to heaven,
So accept the God of truth.

THE LORD BLESS THEE.

"The Lord bless thee and keep thee; the Lord make His face to shine upon thee."

I was very sad and sorrowful, with a weary downcast care,
I wanted much to speak to God, but felt I scarcely dare;

My heart and soul were out of tune, and Satan seemed to be
With all his dangerous, subtle arts, fast triumphing o'er me.

Such little, foolish, trivial acts fretted my spirit sore,
I thought at last I surely was a child of sin once more;
So discontented with the things my God had given to me,
That Satan with his vicious crew were filled with hellish glee.

I wanted everything on earth to be so bright and clear;
I wanted not a single cross to dim my pathway here;
I wanted every one to be so thoughtful, true, and kind,
With friends to soothe and comfort me and ease my troubled mind.

I thought it seemed so hard that I alone should do and bear,
That all my life, and thoughts, and mind, should others burdens share;

You see, I wanted earthly help, and quite forgot my friend,
Who this and every other good, so constantly doth send.

I knew my sin, I felt it every moment of the day,
And I knew the remedy was just to watch and pray;
So took my seat, with fainting heart, and Bible in my hand,
Expecting, surely, there to see, reproof and stern command.

But listlessly I turned it o'er, and thought there's nothing there,
And felt too full of troubled doubt, to offer up one prayer;
But, putting gently back the book, a turned leaf caught my eyes,
I looked to see what might be there, when lo! a glad surprise.

"The Almighty bless thee and keep thee," and further on I read,
"The Lord make His face to shine on thee" in just thy hour of need;

"The Lord be gracious unto thee," when evil powers
  shall cease;
"The Lord lift up His countenance on thee," and give
  thee peace.

Oh! gentle, tender, loving, patient God, how good
  Thou art,
To shed Thy love within my soul, and shew the
  better part;
We come to Thee with all our sins, and faults, and
  wretchedness,
We come to Thee to hear reproof, but only hear Thee
  bless.

And, blessing us with patient love, we come to ask for
  strength,
To bring our crosses all to Thee, whate'er their breadth
  or length;
Assured that we shall lose the weight and burden from
  our mind,
And in the blessed Bible-truths, sweet comfort we
  shall find.

THE NEW NAME.

Oh ! precious Jesus, may Thy name
　Engraven be upon my heart?
That in the anthem of Thy saints,
　I too may take a part.

Oh ! tender Jesus, may Thy name
　Engraven be upon my brow?
That all may know I've learnt of Thee,
　And that Thou'rt with me now.

Oh ! blessed Jesus, may Thy name
　Engraven be upon my hand?
That when life's pleasures come to me,
　I then may firmly stand.

Oh ! loving Jesus, may Thy name
　Engraven be upon my life?
That when life's troubles come to me,
　I may be kept from strife.

Oh! holy Jesus, may Thy name
    Engraven be upon my death?
That all may know I'd come to Thee,
    When I give up my breath.

Oh! righteous Father, may Thy name
    Engraven be upon my soul?
That when the last great trial comes,
    Thou wilt pronounce me whole.

Oh! loving Father, may my name
    Engraven be in Thy dear will?
That in the vast eternity,
    I may be with Thee still

Oh! gracious Father, may my name
    Engraven be in Thy dear love?
That I, the ages yet to come,
    May spend with Thee above.

Oh! "gentle Jesus," when Thou comest,
  In clouds, and power, and bright array,
To fetch Thy ransomed children home,
  Oh! do not bid me stay.

But call me up with loving voice,
  To leave this earth, and meet Thee there;
And then my willing soul will fly,
  To meet Thee in the air.

FEAR NOT, I AM WITH THEE.

Now, in your eyes, I see traces of tears,
And in your heart, there are unknown fears,
  And your head is throbbing with pain;
Just because people are not what they seem,
Just because life is not a mere dream,
  You have lost sight of God again.

Willing to trust Him, in sunshiny hours,
Losing all faith, when tempest lowers,
    No wonder your spirits are low;
Taking such anxious thought for the morrow,
Filling your heart with useless sorrow,
    Just as tho' God did not know

The way you were walking was full of care,
Disappointments more than you could bear,
    If He was not always with thee;
Forgetting that all the hairs of your head
Are numbered, and you are safely led
    The right way your God can see.

Come, take away those sad tears from your eyes,
And fix your hopes on the heavenly prize,
    The Saviour is holding to view;
The way will be dark, if you trust in self,
Or wisdom, or friends, or earthly wealth,
    Or in the works you may do.

Keep your eyes fixed on your heavenly friend,
Think of the joy at the journey's end,
    When the tears will be wiped away;
The night will be past, and trouble all gone,
You'll see the faces of Father and Son,
    Your Father and brother for aye!

THE NEW YEAR.

We've just commenced another year,
    What will this new year bring?
Sorrow and care, and pain and woe,
    Or joy, a glad note ring.

What seemeth best to Thee, my God,
    Is just what I would take;
If joy, I'll praise Thee, but if pain,
    I'll bear it for Thy sake.

And so I'll bring to Thee, again,
  My life, my strength, my all ;
And bending low before Thy throne,
  At Thy dear feet I'll fall.

My future I will trust with Thee,
  And perfect peace secure ;
For Thy word is passed to guide me,
  And Thy promises are sure.

MAMMA, IS THIS THE WAY TO HEAVEN?

Mamma, is this the way to heaven?
The words were gentle, clear, and mild ;
Breathing a tone of earnestness,
And spoken by a little child.

His bright blue eyes, and flaxen curls,
Adorned a face almost too fair
For this world's sin and wickedness,
And weariness, and anxious care.

A quiet, lovely, sunny day,
A lane, which to a valley led;
Scented with new mown hay, and trees,
Which, drooping, nearly met o'er head.

Bright birds were flitting here and there,
The leaves made pleasant murmuring sound,
As though they all had work to do,
To make this earth seem heavenly ground.

The child had heard that heaven was fair,
And calm, and beautiful, and light;
And perhaps he wanted to be there,
Before shut in, again, by night.

It was not much of earth he knew,
He was but just a little boy;
And seemed as tho' his life should be
A gleam of sunshine and of joy.

"Mamma, is this the way to heaven?"
I think I hear the question now;
And, looking down into his face,
She left a kiss upon his brow.

No, Georgie, it is not the way,
The way lies thro' much care and pain;
Not that the trouble you may meet,
Will bring you everlasting gain.

Life is not all a sunny day,
A pleasant stroll, a happy talk;
While flowers and birds, and new mown hay,
Regale the senses while we walk.

Life, means a conflict, fierce and strong,
A battle with the evil one;
But we shall conquer, if we fight,
And trust in Jesus Christ, the Son.

It may be, that Thy path will be
Dark as the darkest midnight here ;
But, with the Saviour's arm around,
There will be nought thou need'st to fear.

So now, dear boy, in after years,
If tempest tossed, and anguish riven ;
Do thou in faith look up, and say,
My God, is this the way to heaven ?

The answer may be, "yes, my child,"
But soon the darkness of the night
Will give place to eternal day,
And floods of everlasting light.

THE ANGEL AND THE CHILD.

Look, at the picture, in this valentine,
It was sent to a little friend of mine,
  One valentine's day.

Well, what is there so wonderful in it?
Do you not see? well, just wait a minute,
    And then you will say

What wonderful love and care there is shown
O'er that dear little child, playing all alone,
    With no one near her.
Watch the loved, little pet, as stooping there,
With her sweet dimpled hands, and curls so fair:
    None can be dearer.

Look, at the flowers, she's gathering up,
Primroses, violets, and sweet buttercups;
    Though she's scarcely fit
To be playing so near the mountain's brink,—
The danger would make her mother's heart sink,
    Could she but see it.

The child knows nothing of danger or fear,
For now, she is drawing awfully near,
    She surely will fall!

Hurrying on, at that fearful rate,
I know it will presently be too late
    For some help to call.

But, stay! see that figure, bending o'er:
Oh! did you not see the angel before?
    With her hands spread out,
Come down from God, on that errand of love,
Quite sure to lift the child up above
    All danger and doubt.

Just so, the same fatherly watchful care,
Is shed o'er our lives, in answer to prayer,
    Before it is prayed.
A look, a sigh, a thought sent to heaven,
Is known there at once, the answer is given,
    And danger is stayed.

How good, our God is, to watch o'er us so,
Keeping sorrow from us, and every foe
    That would do us harm.

And in return may we keep close to Thee,
And feel that from sinful doubt we are free,
    And useless alarm.

Knowing that if we keep close to His side,
The Angel is near, and surely will guide
    Us safe on our way.
Oh! grant we may do the work Thou hast sent,
Nor wilfully wrap up the one talent lent,
    But simply obey.

A CONGRATULATION TO NELLIE.

Well, Miss Nellie, I have just heard,
That you are engaged, my dear;
That Mr. Right has come your way,
And means to steal you, is clear.

I think he has very good taste,
And is exceedingly wise;
And tell him, from me, that I'm sure
He makes good use of his eyes.

He should tender a vote of thanks,
(If he has not done so yet,)
For this new pleasure in life,
To the friends at whose house you met.

I hope you'll be very content,
With the one you each love best;
May the blessing of God descend,
And be your abiding guest.

In the darkest of earth's dark clouds,
If He is within your heart,
He will take away all the pain,
And bid the sorrow depart.

Then, in the sunshiny weather,
When joy fills your heart with love,
He will add to your happiness here,
And point you to realms above.

So, Nellie, I wish you much joy,
In this new path of your life;
And pray that the Father may guide
In your future duties, as wife.

May the one He has given to you,
Nearer, and dearer, still be;
Making your life perfect here,
Is the wish of your friend, F. D.

TO THE SAME, ON HER MARRIAGE.

BEAUTIFUL maiden, bright, and free,
May the birds carol a song for thee;
Telling of happiness, joy, and glee,
On this, thy bridal morning.

Telling of hope, in the future years ;
Taking away from thy heart, all fears ;
Making thee noblest among thy peers ;
    With wisdom thy mind adorning.

Giving thee peace, in thy troubled hours ;
Culling, not weeds, but the sweetest flowers,
In the brightest of earthly bowers,
    With all who are nearest and dearest.
So much, I wish thee, of earthly joy,
Now, for the pleasure, without alloy ;
Now, for faith, which will ever destroy
    All in thy heart, that thou fearest.

Now, thy name's changed, thou'rt free, yet bound ;
May the birds tell as they warble round,
That not one of them fall to the ground,
    Unknown to their Maker, in heaven.

And, if He takes of the birds such care,
Will He not answer thy every prayer,
And the whole weight of thy burdens bear,
   If to Him, thy heart thou hast given?

And watch the birds, when the sun shines bright,
Shouting thanksgiving with all their might;
Praising the loudest, when all is light,
   Their kind Creator above.
Keep near to God, in thy brightest day,
Keep near to Him, when the sun's last ray
Is sinking behind a cloud, it may
   Be the hand of thy Father, in love.

THE NEGLECTED MESSAGE.

IF I had a message to send you,
From a much loved, valued friend;
What would you think of my friendship?
If I had neglected to send.

Especially, if this same message
Referred to some given day,
When they were expecting you there,
Robed in your bridal array.

I might plead that you knew the message,
That you'd heard it once and again,
You'd read it yourself in the letter,
The Bridegroom had made so plain.

I might plead that you'd spoken to me,
That I'd heard you repeatedly say
You meant to accept the invite,
And be there on the marriage day:

Not as a guest, but a child, at home,
With a perfect right to stand,
Surrounded by angels and saints,
One of that glorious band.

Well, I will just remind you, now,
That the time is drawing near;
That you, the dear Father, may meet,
Without the least dread or fear.

And, if I should go home before,
May I tell the Master, that you
Are striving, with all your might,
To follow His footsteps too.

There'll be plenty of sorrow, and pain,
Plenty of trouble, and care;
But, then, there'll be one by your side,
Who, your every trouble will bear.

And, the very short time you are here,
Will seem but a dream, at last,
When you are safe in your Father's home,
And the river of death is past.

But, you see, this invite is different,
From all other bridals I wean;
For, if we are not at the marriage,
We must be at a funeral scene.

The funeral of all our hopes and prayers,
And of every good intent;
When there's no other time to use
The talent the Father lent.

You see, in this, we have nothing to choose,
We must be at the first or the last;
So it rests with ourselves to accept,
Before the great day is past.

So, if you will promise to come,
And let nothing turn you aside,
I will tell them when I go home,
That the gate may be opened wide.

And, perhaps, I may be walking about,
As you are coming up to the gate ;
Then, I will welcome you there,
But, be sure, you are not too late.

For, if once the door should be closed,
No sob, nor tears, nor prayer,
Nor anything we can do,
Will ever avail us there.

PASSING AWAY.

Passing away, from earth to heaven,
Passing away, with our sins forgiven,
   How sweet the message must be.
Passing away, from earth to hell,
Where untold pain and agony dwell ;
   How awful the misery.

Angels hovering round your bed,
Waiting to lay on their bosom your head,
   And carry you home to God.
Demons waiting at your bedside,
Anxious to bear you over the tide;
   Your body laid 'neath the sod.

Lord, in Thy wisdom and wise decree,
Help us to live more nearly to Thee,
   That our lives may please Thee well.
Keep us from sin, temptation, and wrong,
Bid us, in life's dark battle, be strong,
   And keep us, oh! God, from hell.

I WILL TRUST IN THEE.

I AM weary, weary waiting,
   Waiting for the coming day;
When my Lord and Saviour, Jesus,
   Will bear my soul away.

I am thinking, thinking oftimes,
    Oftimes of my home above;
Of the angels, and my Father,
    And its atmosphere of love.

I am listening, listening hourly,
    Hourly for the welcome call;
And I try to paint the moment,
    When I first shall see them all.

I've been reading, reading letters,
    Letters I received of yore;
And I know, too well, the writers,
    Will send to me no more.

But in heaven, in heaven their faces,
    Their faces shine like stars;
And I know I shall go to them,
    When I burst these earthly bars.

So I'm striving, striving fiercely,
   Fiercely with myself and sin ;
And I'm asking that the spirit,
   Will keep me pure within.

For I know, I know I'm sinful,
   Sinful in the sight of God ;
And if He but gave me justice,
   I should sink beneath His rod.

But His tender, tender mercy,
   Mercy sent from heaven, to me :
Blots out all my sinful doings,
   And makes me wholly free.

TO GERALDINE.

A LITTLE, bright-eyed stranger,
   With love in her eye and heart ;
Came into this world of danger,
   In which she must take a part.

May the love of God o'er shield thee,
　　Thou precious, welcome child;
May His right hand uphold thee,
　　As thou passest through the wild.

May His spirit rest upon thee,
　　And crown thy life with love;
Love, not of earth beneath thee,
　　But, love, from heaven above.

Love, that will make thee precious,
　　In a risen Saviour's sight;
Love, that will make thee daring,
　　To ever do the right.

Whate'er thy lot in life my be,
　　Rich, poor, despised, or grand;
Remember, thou'rt a child from heaven,
　　Heiress of heavenly land.

Be thine the lot which Mary chose,
    While in this world thou'lt stay;
Which Jesus Christ, himself, once said,
    Could ne'er be taken away.

And, mayest thou prove, as years pass on,
    With gentle heart, and loving mein,
A truthful, beautious, valentine,
    Strive for the crown, dear Geraldine.

TO A FRIEND, ON HER BAPTISM.

I saw, in her baptismal robe,
    A fair young matron stand;
Waiting, to seal her vow to God,
    One of a little band.

And, as I sat, and watched her, there,
    Her sweet eyes turned to God;
I wondered how much of her life,
    Would pass beneath the rod.

It was pleasant, thus, to see her,
    So rich, so young, so fair;
Give up her life to Jesus Christ,
    While yet so free from care.

Oh! joy to thee, young mother,
    Oh! joy to thee, young wife;
For, now, thy elder brother,
    Can come in to thy life;

And enter into all thy plans,
    And guide thee when in doubt;
And keep thy heart and thoughts all pure,
    And sin, and Satan, out.

Oh! bright the lot thou hast chosen,
    The Saviour's home above;
For the Father's smile is o'er thee,
    And His dear strengthening love.

And now, thy new life's before thee,
    And husband, children, friends,
Will seek to learn the way from thee,
    And all that heavenward tends.

So, keep thee near thy Saviour's side,
    And close to Bible truth;
So shalt thou be a loving guide,
    Of all thy children's youth.

And they will give their hearts to God,
    If faith, and truth, be thine;
And if thy lamp, with steady light,
    Around their feet doth shine.

And, to the rest of that young band,
    Who stood beside thee then;
And gave their hearts and lives to Christ,
    Before assembled men.

One word of warning, and of prayer,
    And sympathy be theirs;
From each of us who witnessed it,
    And offered up our prayers:

That God would ever watch o'er them,
    And guide them in the path,
Of fear, and truth, and rectitude,
    And love of all that hath

Not sin, or love of world in it,
    Nor dread what man may say or do;
If they but work in God's own way,
    And to their own conscience ever true.

So keep you all your fitness for
    The sacred name you share;
For Satan, with consummate art,
    Will bring his skill to bear.

To drag you down from heaven to earth,
    From earth to deeper woe;
And harass, fret, and weary you,
    Till you your faith forego.

But if in times of weakened flesh,
    Or sinful unbelief,
You yield to sin, go back at once
    To God in bitter grief.

And heed you not the tempter's sneer,
    Or Christian's look of scorn;
To seek not God's forgiveness now,
    You had better ne'er been born.

TIMES OF SORROW.

"When thou passeth through the waters, I will be with thee."

The waters are surging high,
And trouble seems coming nigh,
But I to the promise fly,
    And find Thee near.

With a Father's tender heart,
Thou ever wilt take my part,
Nor let the enemies dart
    My soul come near,

And my heart with loving prayer
Would constantly seek Thy care:
So Satan would never dare
    Thy child oppose.
I know sin will be my bane,
Before I my bright home gain,
But Thou wilt soothe all my pain,
    And ease my woes.

I thank Thee, my heavenly friend,
For the trouble Thou dost send,
And making my proud heart bend
    To Thy firm will.

So be the way rough or smooth,
It will still Thy kind love prove,
And nothing shall my heart move ;
    But keep me still

In Thy kind arms till my death,
And then with my latest breath,
I will treasure what Thou saith
    In Thy loved word.
And then with no sob nor sigh,
With the tear for ever dry,—
In my Father's home on high
    I shall see my Lord.

TO NELLIE.

"Set your affection on things above."

I am writing to you, to-day, Nellie,
    And am anxiously waiting to know,
If you are as near to heaven, Nellie,
    As you were some years ago.

For Heaven's so bright and fair, Nellie,
    So perfectly free from pain;
That I'm wanting to see you there, Nellie,
    Surrounded by friends again.

You are young, and you are bright, and you are blithe, Nellie,
    And the friends of this world seem so true;
But I would remind you of one, Nellie,
    Who left dearer friends for you.

And the people He came to save, Nellie,
    Were not His dear friends, you know;
For they heaped upon Him contempt, Nellie,
    And gave Him the bitterest woe.

But the love of His heart never waned, Nellie,
    But faithfully, firmly and kind,
He did the will of His Father, Nellie,
    As He left the desert behind.

And they offered Him worldly wealth, Nellie,
    They would make Him one of earth's kings;
But He knew the void in the soul, Nellie,
    Such short lived pleasures bring.

And pleasures are offered to you, Nellie,
    But oh! don't accept them, my love,
At the price of your precious soul, Nellie,
    Which is anxiously looked for above.

And now that you've a new home, Nellie,
    New duties, new pleasures, new friends;
The old ones never cease praying, Nellie,
    That the talent the Father lends

May be faithfully used by you, Nellie,
    Till the Master comes again;
And however hard the task, Nellie,
    It will bring you the richest gain.

And now for the brightest wish, Nellie,
    My heart can frame or indite :
That the shepherd may keep you safely, Nellie,
    Through the long and dreary night.

May God's spirit rest upon you, Nellie,
    And make you firmly stand,
Till the angels come to carry you, Nellie,
    To the bright and better land.

And once safely within the fold, Nellie,
    You'll never reget the toil,
You had in your Father's service, Nellie,
    While here upon foreign soil.

May the love of the Father rest on thee,
    And the grace of Christ, His Son ;
And the Holy Spirit breathe on thee,
    As thou hearest His own, "well done."

WHY ART THOU CAST DOWN, MY SOUL?

Why art thou cast down, my soul,
    With God so near to thee?
Why let troubled thoughts arise,
    If thou from sin art free?

Did'st thou think on earthly soil,
    That Eden's flowers would bloom;
Or, that earthly joy would light,
    Thy passage to the tomb.

Would'st thou know the source of care,
    And this disquietude:
Look well into thine heart and note
    Its wavering, wandering mood.

Thy thoughts fixed on earthly plans,
    And worldly ways and toys;
And so the spirit leaves thee,
    To taste its empty joys.

Seek again the spirit's aid :
    Back to thy father's arms ;
Then sin for thee shalt have no fear,
    Nor death no dread alarms.

Hope in God and trust in Him,
    And then thou wilt him praise ;
And in the great hereafter,
    The sweetest song shalt raise.

ONLY A BABY, NOTHING MORE.

Only a baby, nothing more ;
But the mother's eyes o'er flowed with tears,
As she looked down at the mourning she wore,
And thought of nights she had battled with fears.

Only a baby, nothing more ;
To that thoughtless tongue and stranger heart :
Little she knew of the heart-strings it tore,
Before its mother with baby could part.

Only a baby, nothing more;
And we turned away with a careless sigh,
Nor ever thought of the anguish they bore,
As the mourning coaches went slowly by.

Only a baby, nothing more;
Ah! me, for the poor sad parents at night:
Turning again to their desolate door,
Entering, gladly would put out all light.

Only a baby, nothing more;
A gift sent by God to brighten this earth,
And lighten the hearts by trouble made sore,
And bring them glad tidings e'n at its birth.

Only a baby, nothing more;
But its little soul has gone back to God!
Its trials and troubles quickly are o'er—
Only its body laid 'neath the sod.

Only a baby, nothing more;
But hark! a glad shout and joy in heaven:
And presently down an angel will soar,
And claim the baby, God has just given.

Only a baby, nothing more;
But look, weeping mother, and dry your eyes.
Tho' only a baby, in sages lore,
'Tis an immortal soul beyond the skies.

Only a baby, nothing more;
But list! to the angels' triumphant song:
While you over baby's trinkets will pore,
Baby is happy in that happy throng.

THE LOSS OF THE PRINCESS ALICE.

IN MEMORIAM.

The loss of the Princess Alice, dear,
Which of the two do you mean?
The wreck of a pleasure steamer,
Or the child of our widowed Queen?

You were playing a game, were you, dear!
And you did not know what to say;
But, darling, it was no game to them,
On that beautiful summer's day.

Yes, both were named Princess Alice,
And both of them lost the same year;
And the sob that ran through the land,
Seems yet to ring in my ear.

Will I tell you the story, little ones?
Yes, if you'll come and sit round;
Curl yourselves up on this cushion,
And put your feet on the ground.

One beautiful, bright sunny day,
Just in the summer time;
When birds were all singing gaily,
And flowers and fruit in their prime;

A great many people were going
On the water to spend the day;
Meaning to be in their homes again,
E'er had sunk the sun's last ray.

Some of them were fathers and mothers,
And would leave their children behind,
To take care of home and each other,
You think it was very unkind.

They did not intend to be so, dear,
They loved their darlings too well;
When they knew they should see them no more,
Their anguish, ah! who may tell.

And the little ones waiting at home,
Till papa and mamma should arrive,
Refusing to credit the story,
They would come home no more alive.

(What are they doing now, did you say?
I am sure I cannot tell;
Their Father, in heaven, is watching,
And He will do all things well.)

There were sisters, and brothers, and friends,
And hundreds of precious lives,
On that doom'd steamer, now sailing in:
But see! how each sailor now strives

To keep out of the way of that ship
That is coming so dangerously near.
The Captain comes up, and calls loudly,
" Where are you coming to here?"

But the great iron Castle came on:
In a moment all was o'er;
The voice which only just now you heard,
Will be heard upon earth no more.

Would they go to heaven, my darlings?
We will leave their souls with God;
But Christians took up their bodies,
And buried them under the sod.

And there was mourning all thro' the land,
And mourning in every face;
And kind hearts wept for others woe,
For the sorrows of their race.

And that was in lovely September,
When the pleasant steamer went down;
No one dreamt of the sorrow in store
For the wearer of England's crown.

But, a murmur went thro' the land,
"The Princess Alice is ill!"
People were almost afraid to ask,
Lest the answer should be worse still.

But the days passed on, and a message came,
She is better, the doctors think;
But then, again, the bulletin read,
She is worse, and likely to sink.

And days went by, and hearts were sad,
As we thought of the loving wife,
And tender mother, whose thought for her child,
Had sacrificed her own life.

And we looked back to her girlish days,
As she stood by her father's bed;
And whispered words of tenderest love,
And soothed his aching, throbbing head.

And later still by her brother's side,
She had come o'er to take her part:
And shower on him in loving care,
The wealth of her thoughtful heart.

I think she had finished her work here,
Meet she should go to her rest;
In tenderest love the angel came:
God always takes those he loves best.

And if only the weeping husband,
And mother, and children will trust,
The gem enshrined to its maker, God,
'Tis only the casket is dust.

The soul has taken its place above,
In the midst of that ransomed throng;
She has learnt the notes the angels sing,
And is helping them sing the song.

Will you strive to be ready, children?
You know not how soon you may go
To the angel's home up in heaven,
Or to sadness, darkness, and woe.

Now, think of the story I've told you,
As suddenly your life may end;
And now in your youth and your beauty,
Oh! make of the Saviour your friend.

IN MEMORIAM.

"Why seek ye the living among the dead?"
   Came into my heart one day,
As I journey'd to see the grave of one,
   Who under the cold sod lay.

My eyes were fixed on the deep blue sky,
   With the white clouds here and there,
Trying to look into heaven beyond,
   And perhaps God took it for prayer.

For my heart was weary, and lone, and sad,—
   I wanted to see my friend:
And receive the welcome I always did,
   When I reached my journey's end.

I knew, tho' I saw her name on the stone,
    I should not see the dear face;
For only strangers would speak to me there,
    And strangers would fill her place.

Who was it that sent the angel to me,
    To tell me she was not dead;
And take the sorrow away from my heart,
    And fill it with joy instead?

now I can see her beyond the grave,
    And Jesus near all the time;
And hark! if you take all your thoughts from earth,
    You will hear the sweet bells chime.

And if you listen, you'll hear them say,
    No sorrow, no death is here;
No sickness, no pain, no parting to bear,
    Nor aught that will cause you a fear.

No darkness, no gas, no need of the sun,
    The sparkling gems will give light;
Adorning the brow of the crucified one,
    Who took from us utter midnight.

I am still on my journey towards the grave,
    But no gloom is there to-day;
The Saviour who sent the message to me,
    Will go with me all the way.

And He'll leave me not, till my heavenly home
    My enraptured soul will see;
And the sainted friends, who went home before,
    Will be there to welcome me.

THE ANSWERED LETTER.

"As thy day is, so shall thy strength be."

WHY need you feel desponding and weary?
When the kind, loving Shepherd is watching o'er you;
What, tho' the way will sometimes be dreary,
If you keep the end of the journey in view.

In the world you will have tribulation and toil,
Loss of health, loss of wealth, and sometimes of friends;
But this should not tend your enjoyment to spoil,
Of the good things your Father so constantly sends.

So far, you've been clothed, and sheltered, and fed,
And things have kept going and coming in, too;
In the past, you have had a home over your head,
And you will have one still if your best you will do.

The little ones God has sent down to your care,
Will cause you expense and anxiety now;
But trained up with thoughtfulness, tenderness, care,
They will smooth care and sorrow away from your brow.

You are sure of protection, watchfulness, love:
God's own word is passed to His children below,—
To send them down help, if they ask from above,
And guide them, and guard them, wherever they go.

The rest you now want will be given you e'er long,—
In the presence of God there is rest ever more;
And you'll join in the glorious triumphant song,
When the troubles and trials of this life are o'er.

You are welcome to sympathy, if it's worth aught:
A recital of trouble ne'er fills me with gloom;
If it soothes your feelings when sometimes o'erwrought,
You may make of your letters, your trouble store-room.

And, as the dear Saviour commanded us here,
To lighten the trouble we meet on our own way;
I would tell you to take from your heart every fear,
And, remember, your strength will be just as your days.

HYMN.

" Jesus, I my cross have taken,"
 And I'll bear it to the grave;
I am faultering, weak, and doubtful,—
 But Thou hast power to save.

Satan comes so often near me,
    Tempting me to leave Thy side;
Showing troubles hovering o'er me,
    Wounding all my earthly pride;

Promising me earthly comforts,
    If I'll join his ranks again;
Shewing riches, wealth, and honour,
    Freedom from all care and pain.

But I've called Thee, "Abba Father:"
    Thou hast called me Thine own child;
And I could not, would not, doubt Thee,
    Tho' the storms blow fierce and wild.

Tho' my flesh is weak and weary,
    My whole heart comes up to Thee;
And I'll bear whate'er Thou willest,
    Tho' I may not, do not, see.

But I'll trust my own dear Father :
    Trust the love that sent His Son ;
Trust Him thro' all times and seasons—
    Trust Him till the crown is won.

Then, when earthly troubles over,
    Christ will take me by the hand :
Lead me up to where the Angels
    Round the throne in glory stand.

Bid me take my place among them,
    And the saints who are there now :
Help them sing the glad hosanna,
    With a crown upon my brow.

Lead me up to where the Father
    Sits upon His glorious Throne :
Tell Him I was always faithful,
    Through the blood of His dear Son.

Then to see the tender welcome
   Beaming from His lips and eye;
Feeling sure to all my struggles
   I have bid a long good-bye.

This will give all faith and comfort,
   Riches that will never end;
So I'll trust Thee, trust Thee only,
   Jesus, Father, truest friend.

GOD'S GREAT LOVE TO MAN.

Some eighteen hundred years ago
There came from heaven to dwell below,
   The holy, tender, Father's Son;
His heart was filled with pitying love:
For looking from His home above,
   He saw the evil we had done.

He knew that God was good and just,
And knew that He must punish us,
   And could not bear the sight.
He left His home so bright and fair,
And came to ours so full of care,
   To save us if he might.

And all along the path He trod,
He left a witness there for God
   To lead us up above.
And when he taught us what to do,
To be so tender, kind and true :
   His text was always love.

Love first our God with all our might,
To do the things we know are right,
   Whate'er our loss may be ;
Then love our neighbour as we would
Be loved by others for our good,
   When we their trouble see ;

Not lightly pass them on the road,
Leave them to bear their heavy load,
   But help them for His sake.
To copy Him in all He did,
To do the things the Scripture's bid,
   Yea! though our hearts may break.

To feel the gentle Father's smile,
Is resting on us all the while,
   Is surely sweetest rest
To know that when our work is done,
We shall be welcomed by the Son,
   And be for ever blest.

With such a bright reward in view,
What is it, Lord, Thou would'st have us do,
   Before we come to Thee.
Oh! lay Thy hand upon our head,
And lead us where we should be led,
   E're we Thy glory see.

GOING HOME.

Going home to Jesus,
But oh! the way seems long;
And sin, flesh, and Satan,
At times appear too strong.

I'm very tired, too,
And weary with earth's care:
But I'll take it all to Jesus,
And leave it there in prayer.

I know He'll send for me,
As soon as he see's fit;
And then good-by to sorrow,
As at His feet I sit.

I'll strive to do His will,
Because I know its right;
I know He'll lead me through
The darkness of the night.

A restful, peaceful ease,
Lost in joy and wonder;
With dear ones all around;
Never more to sunder.

And so I'll bear the pain,
And roughness of the way;
For when the night is past,
Breaks forth eternal day.

IN MEMORIAM.

One more tie in heaven,
    One less here;
Earth is now more dreary,
    Heaven more dear.

One by one they gather
    On the shore;
Freed from toil and sorrow,
    Evermore.

How He gently folds them
    In His flock;
Safe from blighting winter's
    Rudest shock.

As they go in yonder
    From our gaze;
We are lost in sorrow,
    But we'll praise.

For we know our Father,
    And we'er sure
That His gracious promise
    Will endure.

I will never leave Thee
    Nor forsake,
Though Thy dearest treasure
    Thus I take.

You can surely trust them
 To my love ;
They are safely sheltered
 Here above.

Friends may leave and wrong us,
 Bring us woes ;
Not an hidden motive
 But He knows.

And tho' Satan, sneering,
 Says to God :
Take their comforts from them,
 Use the rod :

Then you'll see their goodness
 Pass away ;
But, we'll trust our Father,
 Tho' He slay.

Oh ! I need not tell you
    How the best,
Dearest, of God's children,
    Have a test :

Just to prove to Satan,
    And to say,
We will trust our Father,
    Tho' He slay.

IN MEMORIAM.

On earth, there was sorrow, and weeping, and pain,
But in heaven the joy bells were ringing ;
The angels were tuning their harps afresh,
And the new song lay ready for singing.

A new harp and crown stood ready for use,
And the angels and saints all stood listening,
With words of welcome and love on their lips,
And with gladness their bright eyes were glistening.

For an angel has flown from the upper realms,
With a message from God, on His throne;
To come down with gentleness, pity, and love,
But to take to Him one of His own.

So the angels stood watching the opening door,
'Till the signal be given, and then
They would strike up the harp of glory and praise,
And the loud Alleluia, Amen.

There was sorrow, and pain, and death, with us,
But in heaven it was joyous life;
A freedom from care, temptation, and cross,
And an end of all wearying strife.

We'll think of Thee there, surrounded by love,
In the presence of Father and Son;
We'll meet Thee, again, with joy in our hearts,
When we hear Thee receive the "well done."

And we earnestly ask that God will guide
Our own feet to that land of glory;
When we meet at home we will spend the time,
In rehearsing the old new story.

Then we'll lay our crowns at the Saviour's feet,
And thank Him for partings and weeping;
But for this discipline here upon earth,
This bright harvest we might not be reaping.

GOOD NIGHT.

My darling, I am waiting,
   To hear thy last good night;
And in the morning, when I wake,
   My home will be so bright.

I fancy all the richest things,
   That earth can give to me,
The very least of heaven's gifts,
   Will nobler, grander, be.

I'm waiting for the Master's call,
    And hope it will be soon;
But still I'll wait His gracious will,
    Nor murmur e'er 'tis noon.

And if the darkness of the night
    O'ertake me on the way;
I'll give my hand to Jesus Christ,
    And ever watch and pray.

And so He'll lead me safely on,
    And guide me while I'm here;
If never from His side I roam,
    What can I have to fear?

I know He has given His angels charge,
    Concerning all my life;
And so they'll bear me safely up,
    Thro' joy, and care, and strife.

I'm waiting till the Saviour comes,
    I think He won't be long;
And so, I'll learn, while here on earth,
    The new, the heavenly song.

I know if I draw near in prayer,
    He'll put it in my heart;
And then, when once I've seen His face,
    We never more shall part.

The rain is beating on the pane,
    The wind's wild shriek to-night
Is heard again, and yet again,
    But the morning will be bright.

So I'll say good-bye, at once, dear,
    In case my Father sends,
For I must not keep them waiting:
    Good-bye, my loving friends.

LEAVE THE BLINDS A LITTLE WHILE.

Leave the blinds a little while,
    And take the lights away;
I love to sit in twilight,
    Just at the close of day.

I love to see the shadows
    Lengthening on the ground;
And I like to listen to
    The sweet birds' twittering sound.

And then my eyes go upward,
    To the clear, evening sky;
And dearly I love to watch
    The clouds go sailing by.

I wonder, oh! I wonder,
    If there are people in,
And if their lives are clouded,
    As ours are, here, by sin.

I think they must be angels
    And saints who dwell above;
And they are sent to guard us,
    And watch o'er us in love.

And then the twilight deepens
    Into the evening shades,
And all that's fair and lovely,
    On this earth, quickly fades

From view, but oh! the splendour
    That meets our raptured gaze,
As the stars come peeping out,
    And each one speaks its praise.

And the moon, in all her glory,
    Floods over hill and dale,
And shews the evening beauties,
    That rest on mount and vale.

My heart throbs loud with gladness,
    As stars, and clouds, and moon,
Seem each one coming nearer,
    So I may join them soon.

The evening shades will gather
    Over your life and mine ;
Will twilight hours be welcome ?
    Will glory o'er us shine ?

Shall we gently close our eyes here,
    And wake again in heaven,
And see such glory all around,
    And feel we are forgiven ?

Yes, if we trust in Jesus,
    Our lives will close in Him ;
And the twilight of the evening
    Will bring no shadows dim.

ENTER NOT INTO TEMPTATION.

How beautiful it was,
The few moments He was there;
It came upon me like a dream,
When life was passing fair.

Lost in earthly joy and pleasure,
I was waning in my love,
When an angel left the "Presence,"
With a message from above.

"Enter not into temptation,"
Plainly spoken in my heart;
Then there seemed to be a silence,
And I feared He would depart.

But He stayed a little longer,
And I hoped He'd tell me more;
But the message had been given,
Which I had to ponder o'er.

Still He stayed to give me comfort,
For He knew that I should grieve;
A solemn joy came o'er my soul,
And I scarcely dared to breathe.

I could not speak one word to friends,
Lest the comforter should go;
But the memory of that blessed time
Will cheer my path below.

" Enter not into Temptation ! "
How I pondered what it meant;
And I wondered why my Father
Had from heaven the message sent.

Then I sat, in silence, thinking,
What new danger can be near;
That I need an angel's warning,
When my path seems all so clear.

I thought of all my waywardness,
My carelessness of late;
And I knew I could not lightly
Pass thro' the pearly gate.

My evening hour neglected,
My Bible coldly read,
My prayers just hurried over,
E'er I laid to rest my head.

I thought of all His tenderness,
When He left His home for me;
And the pain and agony He bore,
As He hung upon the tree.

And I wondered if I could not
Give up this world for Him,
If it came between my soul and God,
And made heaven look so dim.

Well, I'll leave it with my Father,
And I know He'll do what's right
And if earth must be darkened,
Heaven will, I know, be bright.

THE JOURNEY OF LIFE.

"Blessed are ye when men shall separate you from their company."

When we left home for the heavenly land,
We thought we would join a nobler band
　Of loving, Christian friends.
So we asked, in our simplicity,
If we might join their company,
　In going the heavenly road.

With loving looks, and winsome voice,
They took our hand and bid us rejoice,
　And glad to have us go.
The Bible says, be lowly and meek,
And never for earthly grandeur seek,
　And we thought it was right.

So we took the blessed book for our guide,
And, by its precepts, meant to abide,
    On our journey through.
But, we were rather surprised to find,
That we were being left behind,
    Or, perhaps before.

It may be in the race for wealth,
God takes away our spirit's health,
    And leaves us poor indeed.
What does it matter, a lowly life,
Filled up with agony, care, and strife,
    If we are near to God?

Friends may mis-judge, and enemies blame,
Sneers and scorn be cast on our name,
    For the Master's sake.
But, leap for joy, the Saviour said,
For richer blessings fall on your head,
    In your heavenly home.

So, whatever loss may betide,
Friends or wealth, keep close to His side,
   And His love will be thine.
And then as we near the heavenly shore,
Earthly distinctions will all be o'er,
   And heavenly love go on.
Only be sure we follow God,
Mark, well, the way His footsteps trod,
   And then be still.

IN MEMORIAM.

One more angel round the throne,
Singing praise to God on high;
But the child is still your own,
Tho' to you she seemed to die.

God but took her from below,
To be free from care and pain;
And when He wants you to go,
You will have her back again.

If you could but see her now,
With a radiance on her face ;
You would at His footstool bow,
Thankful for His loving grace.

It is just to draw you near
To the God you love so well ;
That He took your child from here,
Where He, too, wants you to dwell.

Look not, then, at this dark cloud,
But the silver lining there ;
Tho' you may not ask aloud,
God will hear the whispered prayer.

Take thy sorrow then to Him,
To His sympathising ear ;
And though now thy eyes are dim,
He will check the rising tear.

For, in accents pure and mild,
If you ask you'll hear Him tell;
Is it well with the dear child?
And He'll answer, " it is well."

Oh! His voice will calm thy heart,
And His words will give thee peace;
And an heavenly bliss impart,
Ever more till life shall cease.

FAREWELL TO ENGLAND.

Good-bye, old land, I was going to say, dear,
Perhaps at some future time I may;
But, now, I can spare thee never a tear,
My sun is shining brightly to-day.

Then, perhaps, you will ask, why that yearning look,
Why the tear-drop that dims mine eye?
Ah! those are for friends of whom I just took,
A lingering, loving, final good-bye.

It may be we meet no more upon earth,
And I'm wondering if, when we meet again,
We all shall have passed thro' the second birth,
Or some of us sent to eternal pain.

I am thinking, too, of your gifted land,
Of your Bibles, your churches, your hours of prayer;
And I'm wondering, too, how many will stand,
To receive the robe the churches should wear.

I'm thinking, too, of the class I taught,
Most of their names on the church-book stand;
And I'm praying every name may be placed,
In the glorious book at God's right hand.

When we meet again around the throne,
I shall know, the moment I see them there,
If they have been thoughtful, and earnest, and good,
Or trifled away their hours for prayer.

So tears were for friends I loved so well,
They were kind to me when I needed their love;
And now my highest ambition will be,
To see them with God in their home above.

ANGEL'S VISIT.

An angel came down from heaven one day,
    And laid his hand on my head,
And told me I must be willing to stay,
    Or go where my father led.

It may be thro' depths of deepest woe,
    And sorrow, and care, and pain;
But I must live nearer to God, and so
    I should never feel weary again.

And when discontent came into my mind,
    And I murmured at want of wealth;
He told me to go, some sick one find,
    And ask them what they'd give for my health,

And when I spoke of loneliness, care,
    Which others more favoured had not :
He told me that I could easily share
    With the helpless in some lone cot.

I said if this might be nipped in the bud,
    To anything else I would bend ;
But He told me all would work for my good—
    My Father knew best what to send.

He told me to number my blessings o'er,
    And see if I'd cause to complain ;
And I must be willing to suffer more,
    If it brought me eternal gain.

He tenderly pressed His hand on my brow,
    And winged His way back to heaven :
I felt it then, and I feel it now,—
    Fresh strength to my heart had been given.

'Twas not that He brought me silver and gold,—
  Though I needed both very sore;
He thrilled my soul with the story He told,
  Of the poverty Jesus bore.

He told me to murmur no more while here,
  But bear the cross he had given;
That poverty, pain, sin, sorrow, and death,
  Were things never known in heaven.

JESUS WEPT.

Jesus wept!
Oh! what a solemn sight!
The Lord of earth and heaven,—
The Lord of truth and light,
To be with anguish riven:
Not for His own great loss,
But that his followers must,
For others' lasting good,
In him have perfect trust.

Jesus wept!
Because the friends He lov'd
Were suffering pain and woe!
And He must take no note:
Though He would gladly go
To sooth their care and pain,
And keep the lov'd one here:
And take from heart and mind,
All anguish and all fear.

Jesus wept!
And groaned in spirit, too,
For Lazarus slept.
The Jews stood round with wondering eyes,
And looked on one whom they despised,
With blinded eyes and hardened heart—
They thought in him they had no part.

Jesus wept!
Why should his lov'd ones suffer so?
Why should their heads be bow'd with woe?

Ah! Jesus knew the reason why—
It was that others might not die.

And now they stand around the grave,
Wondering if He had power to save;
And even they who loved Him best
Seemed now to doubt a further test,
Of His almighty power,
In this dread awful hour.

And now a crowd has gathered round,
For well they knew that Lazarus, bound,
Lies in that silent grave below.
But hark! a voice calls loud to heaven,
To thank His Father for strength given,
Time present as in past.

Was there no fear among the crowd,
When they thus heard the voice speak loud:
And saw the dead come forth
In all His burial clothes, and
Napkin wrapp'd around His head?

Some there were who then believed :
Some there were who then received,
And took Him to their heart,
And chose the better part.
Ah ! this was why the Master stayed,
When fain He would have sent them aid
Or some kind loving word.

If in some future of your life ;
If in the midst of some dire strife
You send for Christ to come ;
And if He seem to take no heed,
And come not in thy bitterest need,
What wilt thou do, oh ! soul ?
Doubt Him and think Him hard, unkind !
Doubt him ! whose thought and life and mind
Are centered all on thee !
Or, wilt thou trust and bear the pain,
And know that He will come again,
And weep, when thou do'st weep,
O'er friends not lost—they only sleep.

IN MEMORIAM.
(ACROSTIC.)

Mother's heart was aching sore,
    As they bore thee to the grave;
Round the bier thy kindred stood,
    Trying to be firm and brave.

Hearts would ache and tears would fall,
    As they lowered the coffin down;
As their eyes but saw thee there,
    Never thinking of thy crown.

Now thou art with angels fair,
    Eagerly we scan the sky;
Darling, we would see thee, there,
    And would rest our aching eyes.

Lovingly we speak of thee,
    Though thy life on earth is o'er;
Round the throne a circle see,
    You are there for evermore.

Angels hovering o'er us,
    Greeting us with love;
Ever taking warnings
    Down to those we love.

Sound the trumpet loudly,—
    Ever more shut in;
Vexed no more by Satan,
    Enmity and sin.

Now begins the glory,
    Tranquil pleasure here;
Ever more we're resting,
    Ever Jesus near.

Now, will you not join us,
    Yours the promise, too;
Eagerly we're watching,
    And listening for you.

Rouse thee from thy stupour;
See me as I am;
Oh! give thanks and glory,
Dearest to the Lamb.

TO GRACIE.

"Be thou faithful unto death, and I will give thee a Crown of Life."

Gracie, do you know, my dear,
You have changed your name to day;
But why do you look astonished,
Wondering what it is I say.

Don't you know you are now a Christian,
And your life is not your own;
All the world will now be watching,—
Every action, every tone.

Angels, too, are bending o'er you,
Tending you with anxious care:
Listen to their faithful warnings;
Go for help to God in prayer.

Let the troubles and temptations,
Which beset your path-way here;
Lead you to your home in heaven,
Only bring your Saviour near.

And if wealth should be your portion,
Pleasure gladden all your way;
Still the Master's voice is calling:
Oh! be earnest and obey.

Gracie, won't you work for Jesus?
He has given His life for thine;
He left all so bright and glorious,
That the light round you might shine.

You have taken His Name upon you:
You have made new vows to day;
When God numbers all his jewels,
Wilt thou dwell with Him for aye?

Wilt thou unto death be faithful,
When life's troubles o'er thee come;
When the world looks clothed in darkness,
And with grief thy tongue is dumb.

Will the Crown of Life shine brightly,
When this world shines brightly, too;
Or, will earthly joy and gladness,
Blot the promised land from view.

Oh! be faithful, Gracie, darling,
Life is nothing without God;
Faithful, whatsoe'er He gives you,
Earthly pleasures, or the rod.

MY BIBLE.

My Bible, my Bible, my newly found treasure,
  How I clasp thee with joy to my heart;
Thou art one of my life's very dearest pleasures,
  And in all of it thou shalt have part.

When the sunshine is shedding its glory o'er me,
   I will come to hear what thou wilt say;
When darkness is casting its shadow around,
   Thou wilt shew me, I know, the right way.

I will read thee in sorrow, and anguish and pain,
   When my heart is o'erwhelmed with despair:
I will come very often and read thee again,
   For I know thou wilt take away care.

Thou wilt tell of the beautiful home in the skies,
   Which my Saviour has gone to prepare;
Thou wilt tell me to take from my heart every fear,
   For He'll come back to take me up there.

So the troubles of this life I surely can bear,
   When I know they will work for my good;
In the past I have never known trouble alone,
   By my right side my Saviour has stood.

So my Bible, whene'er disappointment or fear,
    And earth with its sin and its wrong,
Takes hope, joy and gladness, away from my heart,
    Thou wilt point me, I know, to the strong.

LOVE THY NEIGHBOUR AS THYSELF.

"Thou shalt not bear false witness against thy neighbour."

Never speak against thy neighbour—
    Never do a wilful wrong;
God is watching, God is listening:
    Yes they are weak, but He is strong.

No, I know you cannot see Him,
    Neither hear the still small voice;
For your eyes are blind with anger,
    And the very fiends rejoice.

If you could but see them watching;
    If you could but see their leer:
How your heart would stop its beating,
    How your tongue would freeze with fear.

When you've said the worst you can say,
    Not one word you know is true;
But you've gained your end and object,
    And you've worked the mischief, too.

Did you think they had no Brother,
    Who would come and plead their cause?
Did you think they had no Father,
    And you'd broken all His laws?

Did you think He'd take no notice,
    When He saw His children fall?
Or, it may be while you said it,
    That you never thought at all.

But His holy eyes were on you,
    And the evil words you said
Will come back some day with interest,
    And will fall on your own head.

Don't you read in holy Scriptures
    One who made the gallows high;
Falsely, then accusing others,
    But He was the first to die.

STRIVING TO DO THY WILL, OH! GOD.

If I am striving now to be,
A meek, obedient, child to Thee,
And fail again, and yet again,
My God I know it gives Thee pain.

But in my heart I love Thee more,
Than earth with all her wondrous store;
And so I come before Thee now,
And lowly at Thy footstool bow.

To pray that Thou wouldst give Thy hand,
And keep me in Thy chosen band:
And on my forehead put Thy seal,
And all my dire backslidings heal.

When Satan brings temptation near,
And daunts my soul with anxious fear ;
May I to Thy dear refuge fly,
And trust Thee while the dangers high.

IN MEMORIAM.

She was a gentle child,
So patient and mild ;
That the angels, I think,
Thought it scarcely fair,
That one so pure, and tender within,
Should dwell below in this world of sin.

Methinks they had asked of God in His love,
To send for the child to dwell up above ;
And He had seen fit to answer their prayer,
And sent an angel to take her up there.

But the father's heart ached,—
And the mother wept ;
They could not remember
Their darling but slept,

To wake up in glory in heaven;
Where a golden crown would be given,
And a robe, spotless, and pure, and white,
And her companions all angels of light.
Mamma's gentle lamb was safe in the fold,
Never again to feel pain, heat, or cold.

  The bells rang out loud,
  For never a cloud
  Fell on any one's heart,
  In that peaceful land:
For none but the holy e'er came;
They knew the watch-word—Jesu's name.

  Then why do you weep?
  The Saviour will keep
Your little one safe till you go—
To meet in that land free from woe.

  Beautiful and bright,
  Fairer than the light,
Will your little daughter wait,
Your entrance through the pearly gate.

THE SECRET OF THE LORD.

I've often wondered what it is,
    The secret of the Lord;
I've sat and thought and pondered o'er,
    His precious treasured word.

I've thought sometimes I'd found it out,
    But then I was not sure;
'Tis only given to those whose lives
    And thoughts are all quite pure.

But then I've thought there are none good,
    Save God Himself, not one:
For this was said some centuries back,
    By His beloved Son.

'Tis given to those who fear our God:
    Not slavish fear, you know;
But fear to grieve Him any way,
    Because they love Him so.

WORK FOR THE WOMEN OF ENGLAND.

I wonder if anything short of a plague,
    Would stem this torrent of drink?
I wonder if anything short of grim death,
    Would teach us to pause and think?

Short of death, did I say! they are dying by scores,
    Slain down by remorseless hand:
And the blood of their guilt lies close to our doors,
    The doors of a Christian band.

We pity the plague spot, we shudder and shrink,
    As we pass the drunkard by;
But we put not our hand out to shew them the right,
    But leave them to drink and die!

We fain would do something for God and for man,
    If friends would smile on our way;
But a frown, a look, a discouraging word,
    Drives us from duty away.

Oh! fathers and brothers, oh! husbands and sons,
    Has this curse fallen on you?
Be gentle and tender in bringing them back:
    Yourselves be manly and true.

Oh! mothers and sisters, oh! daughters and wives,
    If careless and thoughtless you've been:
Do strive in the future to save the dear lives—
    The life of their souls, I mean.

When the table is spread, and the glittering glass
    Is filled for your hand to take,
To pass on to sister, son, husband, or friend,
    Put it down, for Jesu's sake.

The sarcastic smile, the side scornful glance,
    Will be hard, I know, to bear;
But it may be you'd wish you'd taken that cross,
    Than this one of anxious care.

When your husband, your mother, your father, your son,
    Alas ! even worse it may be :
The child of your love, the bright, beautiful girl,
    You find from this taint is not free.

Too late is the warning, too late is the prayer :
    You shudder, your heart may break ;
The meaningless look, the half foolish laugh,
    Ah ! hide them for pity's sake.

Or it may be the light will fade from your eyes,
    Your heart throb loudly with fear,
As the sound of the voice, and the step once so loved,
    Falls sadly now on your ear.

And the hand, which was once raised only to bless,
    Falls now with dull heavy smart ;
And the fearful words you'r listening to,
    Takes the last hope from your heart.

Oh! mothers of England, be yours the good work,
   Whatever the past may have been;
Do not let your child taste, whatever the cost,
   And let your own hands be clean.

And the day will dawn, the bright, beautiful day,
   When drunkards will never be known;
And the curse of our land, our Bible read land,
   For ever, and ever, o'erthrown.

THE BLUE RIBBON ARMY.

We're the Blue Ribbon Army, just sworn in
      To obey our King;
And the very best of everything we have in life,
      We are going to bring.

First, we bring Him blooming health and strength,
      And lay at His feet;
And promise we'll use heart and voice against
      Every foe we meet.

We are going to try what we can do
    For the Temperance cause;
And we want you all to help us, will you?
    To obey the laws.

Some of you will say you are much too young,
    And others too old;
But we'll tell you each what your work will be,
    If you will be told.

We want to tell the little boys and girls
    They can join us here;
But they must be prepared for sacrifice,
    But they need not fear;

For our Captain always stands by our side,
    And shows us the way;
With such a glorious leader, don't you think
    We shall win the day?

Of course, we shall have to fight very hard,
    And get many blows;
But we are not expecting beds of roses
    In the midst of foes.

First, if you are offered a glass of wine,—
    "Thank you," with a bow:
"But I've joined the Blue Ribbon Army,
    I do not take it now."

Then, we've Temperance books we want to fill,
    Shall I write your name?
I should like to have it down in my list,
    It will add to your fame.

For we want you so much to share with us
    The heavenly prize,
The Saviour is holding up to view
    Before your eyes.

For the words are dreadful, dreadful to hear,—
    Drunkards, come not in ;
Oh ! God, take from us this curse of our land,
    And all other sin.

JUST TEN O'CLOCK ON A SABBATH EVE.

" Remember the Sabbath day to keep it Holy."

Just ten o'clock, on a Sabbath eve,
And everything quiet and still ;
The working day sounds had ceased for a time,
And hushed was the whir of the mill.

So still, and so calm, so free from care,
It seemed just the time to meet God ;
And ask for new strength for the coming week,
And, perhaps, to bend 'neath the rod.

The hour was pleasant, and holy, and prized,
As hours spent with God ever are ;
When, suddenly, sounds recalled me to earth,
With a not very pleasant jar.

A shuffling footstep, a mumbling noise,
A voice, surely trying to utter
Some articulate sound to someone or himself,
Just proved inarticulate mutter.

But now, a firm and decided step,
Stops to ask where the man would roam;
And a voice of pity, but firmness said,
" Don't you think you had better go home?"

I pictured the home he was going to,
Full of care, want, sorrow, and pain;
I pictured his wife, mother, children,
So anxiously waiting again.

The sounds died away, the street seemed clear,
And I foolishly thought all were gone;
Till a hideous clatter of feet told me nay,
And a voice, loud and hoarse, screamed, "come on."

Where to ! would he pause and think ?
E'er he walked on such dangerous ground ;
Would the demon drink blind his eyes for aye ?
And revit the chains he had bound

Him, body and soul, with such fiendish glee,—
A soul, for which Jesus died ;
And coward-like we shrink from our task,
And say its no use before we have tried.

One soul for Jesus, one saved from sin,
Will be worth all the work we can do ;
And if only one comes o'er to our side,
I shall work with fresh courage, will you ?

WHO IS TO BLAME?

"No drunkard can enter the kingdom of heaven."

No drunkard can enter the kingdom of heaven,
   But what does a drunkard mean ?
Is it one who tumbles o'er all he comes near,
   Or, only one who need lean ?

You know there are some who drink glass after glass,
    With no bad effects at all;
And if others but take the very least cup,
    Were they not helped, they would fall.

I read in the papers, the other day,
    Of a lady young and fair,
Whose peculiar walk, and reeling form,
    Caused each one to turn and stare.

And a crowd of rough boys and men gathered round,
    And jeered as she passed along;
Till a gentleman* went, and spoke to her there,
    And took her out of the throng.

It was long before she could tell where she lived,
    Or how she came in that state;
It appears she had been to visit her aunt—
    Had some little time to wait.

            * Mr. Gough.

And her aunt, good natured, and foolish withal,
    Pursuaded her just to drink
" The least drop of whiskey and water, just warm ;
    " It will do you good, I think."

And the poor child not being used to such stuff,
    Took the glass from her relative's hand ;
Then found as soon as she went in the air,
    She had not the power to stand.

That raises another question, you see ;
    I think they are most to blame,
Who offer the wine glass to those who call,
    Who ne'er drank before they came.

I know you will say, they've their own free will,
    They need not touch if they choose—
To put down the glass, they are welcome to do,
    They only need to refuse.

But the custom, my friend, ah! custom is strong,
    And they dare not raise a laugh;
So against their conscience and judgment both,
    The poisonous drink they quaff.

But the day is coming, and will not be long,
    When custom will turn quite round;
And the fetters of drink, which are now so strong,
    Will quietly slip to the ground.

And then, when we go to meet God in prayer,
    And tell Him we are seeking to find
Some poor lost drunkard, we'll bring him, and say,
    " Here, Lord, and in their right mind."

THE HIDDEN PATH.

I'm just in deep perplexity,
    And cannot see my way at all;
My path seems dark, or blotted out,
    I dare not move lest I should fall.

What seem'd so clear and bright, this morn,
Is wrong and wearying now, to me;
And yet I know the hidden path,
Thy own dear eyes can plainly see.

Then why this fear, and thought, and care?
When every moment of my life
Is planned by Thee, and Thou wilt lead
Me safe amid the world's dark strife.

And, so, I'll move on step by step,
Sure that Thy hand will safely lead
From light to dark, from dark to light,
Tho' I Thy purpose cannot read.

I know it is to clear the dross,
And take the evil from my heart;
That when I stand before Thy throne,
Thou wilt not say to me, "depart."

And, so, however dark the way,
I trust in Thee to lead me on;
And never falter while Thou'rt near,
Save in the blood of Christ, Thy Son.

MAMMA, I SAW YOU; AUNTY, SHALL I SEE JESUS?

WHAT meant the exclamation,
  "Mamma, I saw you then!"
And why the joyful answer,
  "Did you," my darling, "when?"

You went across the room, Ma,
  I saw your face quite plain,
And I was glad, so glad, Ma,
  To see you once again.

What dress have I on, Sissie?
  Ah! that I do not know;
I only saw your face, Ma,
  I did not look below.

I did not think about your dress,
    I wanted so to see
The dear face and eyes, Mamma,
    That used to look at me.

And now I want to see Pa,
    And little Sissie, too;
And Aunty, I dearly wish,
    I only could see you.

Shall I see Jesus, Aunty,
    When I go up to heaven?
Will he speak to little girls,
    Who are but just turned seven?

Or, are they only angels,
    Whom Jesus speaks to, there;
And shall I be an angel?
    And, Aunty, shall I wear

White princess robes there all the time?
    And will the angels see—
I want so much to learn to play
    The harp just given to me!

Ah! Sissie, you have learnt it all,
    Much more than Aunty knows;
You've learnt the song, you've learnt the harp,
    And from your tongue now flows

The joyful anthem of the blest
    And saved, who live above,—
Of children of the heavenly King,
    Whose lives are full of love.

Fit you should wear a princess robe:
    The daughter of a King
Is robed in white, all gloriously,
    And beautiful within.

IN MEMORIAM.

We laid her in the grave, but yesterday,
And left her in the deep, cold, silent ground,
With none but dead to keep her company,
And they lay, thickly scattered all around.

And we went home to think, and sob, and cry,
And wonder what the meaning of this cross;
And murmur that the one we loved should die,
And mourn and wail, o'er this, our bitter loss.

And God and heaven seemed very far away,
So far, we could not see the loved one there;
And so we knelt in silence, dumb, to pray,
And God just listened to the unspoken prayer.

And tho' He did not tell the dead to rise,
As Lazarus did, to life, and strength, and health;
He gave us faith to see with human eyes,
The deep, unspoken, boundless love and wealth,

Which now were hers, her own for evermore,—
Nor sin, nor sorrow, pain, could touch her now;
And as we looked, we saw the robe she wore,
Spotless and white, and crown upon her brow.

And as we looked, we thought of all the pain
And cries of anguish she had uttered here:
And how we stood around her bed, and fain
Would help and sooth the one to us dear.

And still we looked, and wondered how our God,
So tender, pitying, Fatherly and kind,
Should make His children pass beneath the rod,
E're they in heaven, their resting place should find.

And still we looked, and saw them round the throne,
Spotless and pure, radient, bright and fair;
And thought of her who once was all our own,
Ah! still our own, tho' higher love she'll share.

But still we wondered, till an angel came,
And saw our deep perplexity, and said :
She is from earth, but here she's changed her name,
She still is living, tho' you thought her dead;

She's dead to earth, but hark ! she speaketh yet
To you below in sorrow, joy and peace ;
Her life will speak, if you will only let
The voice be heard, when years and wealth increase.

We rose from bended knees, with lightened heart,
Thankful for God's great gift, His only Son ;
Resolved that with His help we'd do our part,
And bear the cross, and sing the Victory is won.

WHY DID YOU GIVE UP YOUR SCHOOL?

Why did you give up your school ?
I did not, it gave up me ;
Yes, it was trouble enough,
The future I could not see.

'Twas dark, as the darkest night,
   Not a star shone on my way;
I wondered if I should see
   The dawn of a coming day.

It was not for very long,—
   I just looked up above,
And saw thro' the lowering clouds,
   The proof of my Father's love.

One smile from His loving face,
   Just flooded my soul all o'er;
I could see the reason why,
   And it was not dark any more.

I should have to live by faith:
   A lesson I needed much;
So I put my hand in His,
   And asked Him to teach me such.

As He saw I needed most
    While I dwelt a pilgrim here;
And shew me that perfect love
    Would surely cast out all fear.

So I'm walking, now, by faith,
    And it is not dark at all;
And now I have time to list
    To the Saviour's welcome call.

So I did not give up my school,—
    The Master took it away:
He'd told me before to come,
    But I had not thought to obey.

He quietly spoke the word,
    And blotted it out from view:
And gave me to understand,
    I had other work to do.

So I'm working now very hard,
    At the work my soul loves best;
And I want to finish my task,
    Before I go home to rest.

WILL YOU WRITE A PIECE FOR MY ALBUM?

What must I write in your album?
What must the tenor and tone of it be?
Merry and glad, mournful and sad:
Will you strike the note, and give it to me.

Must I write of the future years,
Brightness and happiness, without alloy;
Sunshine, no rain, freedom from pain,
And all that this world can think of as joy.

Must I picture a cosy home,
With one, whom you love, in the easy chair;
Thoughtful and kind, just of your mind,
With never a trouble or cross to bear.

What more is there left me to tell?
What more is there left me to wish for you?
Unfading health, unbounded wealth,
Friends, who will ever be faithful and true.

If I had the power to give
Health, wealth, friends, and ease in this happy home,
And you had this unfading bliss,
Don't you think it would tend to make you roam

From your heavenly home in the skies?
Your thoughts would be centred and fixed on earth :
Near to the brink, your heart would sink ;
If an angel came, in the midst of mirth,

And brought you a summons to go,
In the midst of health, and pleasure, and love,-
No time to wait, enter the gate,
Of a land of woe, or a land above.

What must I write in your album?
Must I tell of the joy which in Jesus lives?
Peace in your heart, heals every smart,
And joy will be lasting, which Jesus gives.

I'll write one wish in your album:
The talent, the Master gives, may be used;
Not wrapped away, from day to day,
Thoughtlessly, wilfully, surely misused.

I wish you an unfading crown,
Whatever your troubles and happiness here:
Harp in your hand, a right to stand
In the home of God, without any fear.

I wish you acceptance through Christ,
Through the death of the Father's dearest Son;
Keep close to Him, tho' with eyes dim,
Receive, in return, the Father's " well done."

THE THORN IN THE FLESH.

"He sent them flesh, but he sent them leanness into their souls."

I'd a cross to bear, a thorn in the flesh,
And it fretted and chafed me every day;
I thought I should like to choose my own cross,
If only this might be taken away.

I had health, and joy, and peace in my heart,
Notwithstanding the cross that pressed me then;
An angel from heaven stood close to my side,
And seemed to know, just the how and the when,

It would be too heavy for me to bear:
So just moved his hand, and lifted it up,
And lightened the burden: and if I seemed faint
Would whisper to me, "Christ drank of this Cup."

And it seemed to put new life in my soul,
To remember what Jesus had done for me;
How he'd taken the veil away from my eyes,
And given me wonderful things to see.

I don't think I murmured so much as I thought,
If I had not this cross I should not have one;
And I did not remember that while upon earth,
I must have a cross till my work was done.

But the Master thought I should have my way,
So took the thorn away from my life;
But He took His strength, and grace away, too,
And left me alone in the world's dark strife.

And now I had gold, bright, glittering gold,
Which was to act the magician's part:
But I'd scarcely taken it up in my hand,
Before the "happy" went out of my heart;

And a dull, heavy weight, fell on my soul,
And I seemed to feel like a stranger here;
With none to comfort, or stand by my side,
And my heart was filled with an unknown fear.

I think I had chosen to choose my cross,
And now I'd not one, but many, to bear ;
With never a gleam of light from heaven,
Nor angel was sent my burden to share.

First, came misunderstanding with friends.
Which kept me awake for a night or two :
I felt, I was sure, I was not in the wrong,
And I could not make up my mind what to do.

Then came affliction, with its darkening wing,
And put new sorrow, and care, in my heart,
By laying its hand upon one I loved,
And threatening body and soul to part.

Darkness, and trouble, and sorrow, and pain :
No God to go to, no comforter now ;
I wondered, indeed, how much I had,
As I wiped cold drops away from my brow.

But my God was near, and watching me, too,
Tho' He'd hidden His light from me awhile,
He knew well His wayward, wandering child,
Could not live upon earth, without His smile.

So I went back to Him, and asked if He
Would forgive the murmuring discontent,
And make me more willing to bear His will,
And send back the cross, He once had sent.

And He was not like earthly friends at all,
No sarcastic smile on His face was seen ;
But a tender, gentle, pitying love,
As He quietly shewed me, what might have been.

He took back the cross, and gave me my own,
The one He knew well for me was best ;
And sent back His angel, and strength, and grace,
And calm, unspeakable, infinite rest.

CONCLUSION.

Dear Reader, I'm sending this book to you,
Hoping that if you should read it quite through:
For all in it, good and holy, you see,
Give the glory to God, and not to me.

And all in it wrong, and worthy of blame,
As my share of the book, I simply claim;
If you approve, when you come to the end,
Will you kindly mention to neighbour and friend.

www.ingramcontent.com/pod-product-compliance
Lightning Source LLC
Chambersburg PA
CBHW030339170426
43202CB00010B/1178